Poems for Children

To Alasdair
Christmas 2001
love
Mummy
+ Daddy
x x

TOM HUBBARD is a poet, scholar and editor who has taught at a number of overseas universities. From 1984 to 1992 he was librarian of the Scottish Poetry Library, and is currently editor of BOSLIT, the on-line Bibliography of Scottish Literature in Translation, based in the National Library of Scotland. He has previously edited a selection of William Soutar's poems for children, *A Bairn's Sang*, for Mercat Press; this Stevenson selection is part of the same series. His 10-year-old daughter, **CLAIRE**, has helped to choose the poems for both the Soutar and Stevenson titles. She is a pupil at Kirk-caldy West Primary School, and enjoys writing and drawing.

POEMS FOR CHILDREN

ROBERT LOUIS STEVENSON

edited by
Tom and Claire Hubbard

with illustrations by
Sheila Cant

MERCAT
PRESS

This edition first published in 2000 by Mercat Press
James Thin, 53 South Bridge, Edinburgh EH1 1YS

Introduction and glossary © Tom and Claire Hubbard, 2000

Illustrations © Sheila Cant, 2000

ISBN: 184183 0143

Typeset in Footlight MT Light at Mercat Press
Printed and bound in Great Britain by
Redwood Books, Trowbridge, Wiltshire

CONTENTS

INTRODUCTION

Robert Louis Stevenson lived in many countries but he always remembered his native Scotland; he loved to travel but that didn't stop him feeling homesick whenever he was abroad. Actually, the word 'home' sounds a bit odd when we think of Robert Louis Stevenson. Many people live in one house in one town for much of their lives; that wasn't the case with him. He was a man on the move.

Stevenson collected most of his poems for young people in the book *A Child's Garden of Verses*, and in the following pages we've included some of the most popular poems from that book. Many of them draw on his memories of his own childhood in Edinburgh, where he was born in 1850. Throughout his life he suffered from ill health; it often happens that very sick children have to pretend to do the fun things which are impossible for them in real life. At bedtime he was told exciting but terrifying stories from Scottish history and legend. (Scottish stories tend to be pretty scary, one way or the other.) The result was night after night of dreams about mysterious horsemen riding furiously in the dark, about having to swallow the whole world in one gulp (what had they given him for supper?) and so on. Of course he'd wake up screaming. (Did I say 'fun things' a few lines back?!) However, all this stuff excited his imagination and he went on to write some of the world's best tales of the supernatural.

The 'Edinburgh and Scotland' section of this book includes the poem 'Keepsake Mill', which was inspired by the village of Colinton just outside Edinburgh. He played here as a boy, not far from his grandfather's house. Stevenson also loved the wilder parts of Scotland, and we've chosen a couple of poems about the Highlands, including 'The Song of the Sword of Alan', which fascinated us because it sounded so strange. Stevenson originally included this poem in *Kidnapped*, one of his best-loved adventure stories.

The house at Colinton was full of mysterious objects from India. From his parents' house in Edinburgh he enjoyed a view of the Forth estuary which flows into the North Sea. He wondered about the world beyond, and as he grew older it became clear that he wasn't going to let poor health get in the way of his passion for travel and adventure. His love of the sea also owes a lot to the fact that the Stevenson family had been lighthouse engineers—he was fascinated by lighthouses, built on remote rocks, inhabited by lonely men whose work prevented many a possible shipwreck. No wonder he went on to write about the dangers experienced by sailors—and pirates.

In his late twenties Stevenson boarded a crowded ship bound for New York, and endured a rough train ride right across America. His purpose was to join the San Francisco lady whom he had met a few years earlier in France, and to marry her. What a romantic! (By the way, his wanderings in France had included a camping trip in the wild mountain country of the south, in the company of a donkey called Modestine, who carried his equipment on her back: see the poem 'A Camp'.)

During his Scottish childhood Stevenson loved islands—we have a lot of them in our country. Even a patch of ground in the middle of a pond or a stream could have him dreaming up the most colourful characters and events. Many of us have enjoyed drawing maps of places that don't exist; the most famous example is the map which illustrates *Treasure Island*, the first book which made Stevenson famous.

Stevenson and his family eventually left America for the Pacific islands. They made their home in Samoa, where Stevenson continued to write about Scotland as well as about his new surroundings. It was there, in 1894, that he died, suddenly, aged only 44.

Stevenson never lost his love of play. Once, when the family was living in Switzerland, he and his young stepson Lloyd bought a small printing press. They made woodcuts which they used to illustrate the little poetry books that they produced under such titles as *The Graver and the Pen*, *Moral Emblems* and *Moral Tales*. We've included some of the poems (with the original illustrations) from these booklets; they're not as serious as they appear to be at first.

Most people think of Stevenson as a storyteller rather than as a poet, so it's not surprising that in many of his poems he can't resist telling a story. A friend of mine was delighted when I told him that Claire and I had decided to include 'Ticonderoga' in our book; he told me that he thought it was a great poem to read aloud. I think it's also a poem that has so many of the ingredients of the Stevenson 'flavour': it's mysterious, even supernatural; it takes place in more than one country and yet has its beginnings in Scotland. We hope that our book will give you an idea of Stevenson's love of foreign lands, but also a taste of the country which he saw for the last time seven years before his death, the country which he never forgot when he was living at the other side of the world.

Tom Hubbard

1
EDINBURGH
AND
SCOTLAND

The Lamplighter

THE LAMPLIGHTER

My tea is nearly ready and the sun has left the sky;
It's time to take the window to see Leerie going by;
For every night at teatime and before you take your seat,
With lantern and with ladder he comes posting up the
      street.

Now Tom would be a driver and Maria go to sea,
And my papa's a banker and as rich as he can be;
But I, when I am stronger and can choose what I'm to do,
O Leerie, I'll go round at night and light the lamps with
      you!

For we are very lucky, with a lamp before the door,
And Leerie stops to light it as he lights so many more;
And oh! before you hurry by with ladder and with light;
O Leerie, see a little child and nod to him to-night!

KEEPSAKE MILL

Over the borders, a sin without pardon,
    Breaking the branches and crawling below,
Out through the breach in the wall of the garden,
    Down by the banks of the river we go.

Here is a mill with the humming of thunder,
    Here is the weir with the wonder of foam,
Here is the sluice with the race running under—
    Marvellous places, though handy to home!

Sounds of the village grow stiller and stiller,
    Stiller the note of the birds on the hill;
Dusty and dim are the eyes of the miller,
    Deaf are his ears with the moil of the mill.

Years may go by, and the wheel in the river
    Wheel as it wheels for us, children, to-day,
Wheel and keep roaring and foaming for ever
    Long after all of the boys are away.

Home for the Indies and home from the ocean,
    Heroes and soldiers we all shall come home;
Still we shall find the old mill wheel in motion,
    Turning and churning that river to foam.

You with the bean that I gave when we quarrelled,
    I with your marble of Saturday last,
Honoured and old and all gaily apparelled,
    Here we shall meet and remember the past.

AULD REEKIE

When chitterin' cauld the day sall daw,
Loud may your bonny bugles blaw
    And loud your drums may beat.
Hie owre the land at evenfa'
Your lamps may glitter raw by raw,
    Along the gowsty street.

I gang nae mair where ance I gaed,
By Brunston, Fairmileheid, or Braid;
But far fraw Kirk and Tron.
O still ayont the muckle sea,
Still are ye dear, and dear to me,
Auld Reekie, still and on!

IN THE HIGHLANDS

In the highlands, in the country places,
Where the old plain men have rosy faces,
And the young fair maidens
Quiet eyes;
Where essential silence cheers and blesses,
And for ever in the hill-recesses
Her more lovely music
Broods and dies.

O to mount again where erst I haunted;
Where the old red hills are bird-enchanted,
And the low green meadows
Bright with sward;
And when even dies, the million-tinted,
And the night has come, and planets glinted,
Lo, the valley hollow
Lamp-bestarred!

O to dream, O to awake and wander
There, and with delight to take and render,
Through the trance of silence,
Quiet breath;
Lo! for there, among the flowers and grasses,
Only the mightier movement sounds and passes;
Only winds and rivers,
Life and death.

THE SONG OF THE SWORD OF ALAN
From *Kidnapped*

This is the song of the sword of Alan:
The smith made it,
The fire set it;
Now it shines in the hand of Alan Breck.

Their eyes were many and bright,
Swift were they to behold,
Many the hands they guided:
The sword was alone.

The dun deer troop over the hill,
They are many, the hill is one:
The dun deer vanish,
The hill remains.

Come to me from the hills of heather,
Come from the isles of the sea.
O far-beholding eagles,
Here is your meat.

2
PEOPLE

The Industrious Pirate

A PORTRAIT

I am a kind of farthing dip,
    Unfriendly to the nose and eyes;
A blue-behinded ape, I skip
    Upon the trees of Paradise.

At mankind's feast, I take my place
    In solemn, sanctimonious state,
And have the air of saying grace
    While I defile the dinner plate.

I am 'the smiler with the knife,'
    The battener upon garbage, I—
Dear Heaven, with such a rancid life,
    Were it not better far to die?

Yet still, about the human pale,
    I love to scamper, love to race,
To swing by my irreverent tail
    All over the most holy place;

And when at length, some golden day,
    The unfailing sportsman, aiming at,
Shall bag, me—all the world shall say:
    Thank God, and there's an end of that!

ON SOME GHASTLY COMPANIONS
AT A SPA

That was an evil day when I
To Strathpeffer drew anigh,
For there I found no human soul
But Ogres occupied the whole.

They had at first a human air
In coats and flannel underwear.
They rose and walked upon their feet
And filled their bellies full of meat.
They wiped their lips when they had done
But they were Ogres every one.

Each issuing from his secret bower,
I marked them in the morning hour.
By limp and totter, lisp and droop,
I singled each one from the group.
I knew them all as they went by—
I knew them by their blasted eye!

Detested Ogres, from my sight
Depart to your congenial night!
From these fair vales, from this fair day,
Fleet, spectres, on your downward way,
Like changing figures in a dream,
To Muttonhole or Pittenweem!
As, by some harmony divine
The devils quartered in the swine,
If any baser place exist
In God's great registration list—
Some den with wallow and a trough—
Find it, ye ogres, and be off!

THE ANGLER ROSE, HE TOOK HIS ROD

The angler rose, he took his rod,
He kneeled and made his prayers to God.
The living God sat overhead:
The angler tripped, the eels were fed.

THE ANGLER AND THE CLOWN
From *The Graver and the Pen*

The echoing bridge you here may see,
The pouring lynn, the waving tree,
The eager angler fresh from town—
Above, the contumelious clown.
The angler plies his line and rod,
The clodpole stands with many a nod—
With many a nod and many a grin,
He sees him cast his engine in.

'What have you caught?' the peasant cries.

'Nothing as yet,' the Fool replies.

JAVELIN IN ABBOT
From *Moral Emblems*

The Abbot for a walk went out,
A wealthy cleric, very stout,
And Robin has that Abbot stuck
As the red hunter spears the buck.
The djavel or the javelin
Has, you observe, gone bravely in,
And you may hear that weapon whack
Bang through the middle of his back.
Hence we may learn that abbots should
Never go walking in a wood.

INDUSTRIOUS PIRATE!
From *Moral Emblems*

Industrious pirate! see him sweep
The lonely bosom of the deep,
And daily the horizon scan
From Hatteras or Matapan.
Be sure, before that pirate's old,
He will have made a pot of gold,
And will retire from all his labours
And be respected by his neighbours.
You also scan your life's horizon
For all that you can clap your eyes on.

THE SPAEWIFE

O, I wad like to ken—to the beggar-wife says I—
Why chops are guid to brander and nane sae guid to fry.
An' siller, that's sae braw to keep, is brawer still to gi'e.
—*It's gey an' easy spierin'*, says the beggar-wife to me.

O, I wad like to ken—to the beggar-wife says I—
Hoo a' things come to be whaur we find them when we try,
The lasses in their claes an' the fishes in the sea.
—*It's gey an' easy spierin'*, says the beggar-wife to me.

O, I wad like to ken—to the beggar-wife says I—
Why lads are a' to sell an' lasses a' to buy;
An' naebody for dacency but barely twa or three
—*It's gey an' easy spierin'*, says the beggar-wife to me.

O, I wad like to ken—to the beggar-wife says I—
Gin death's as shure to men as killin' is to kye,
Why God has filled the yearth sae fu' o' tasty things to pree.
—*It's gey an' easy spierin'*, says the beggar-wife to me.

O, I wad like to ken—to the beggar-wife says I—
The reason o' the cause an' the wherefore o' the why,
Wi' mony anither riddle brings the tear into my e'e.
—*It's gey an' easy spierin'*, says the beggar-wife to me.

MY WIFE

Trusty, dusky, vivid, true,
With eyes of gold and bramble-dew,
Steel-true and blade-straight,
The great artificer
Made my mate.

Honour, anger, valour, fire;
A love that life could never tire,
Death quench or evil stir,
The mighty master
Gave to her.

Teacher, tender comrade, wife,
A fellow-farer true through life,
Heart-whole and soul-free
The august father
Gave to me.

IT IS NOT YOURS, O MOTHER

It is not yours, O mother, to complain,
Not, mother, yours to weep,
Though nevermore your son again
Shall to your bosom creep,
Though nevermore again you watch your baby sleep.

Though in the greener paths of earth,
Mother and child, no more
We wander; and no more the birth
Of me whom once you bore,
Seems still the brave reward that once it seemed of yore;

Though as all passes, day and night,
The seasons and the years,
From you, O mother, this delight,
This also disappears—
Some profit yet survives of all your pangs and tears.

The child, the seed, the grain of corn,
The acorn on the hill,
Each for some separate end is born
In season fit, and still
Each must in strength arise to work the almighty will.

So from the hearth the children flee,
By that almighty hand
Austerely led; so one by sea
Goes forth, and one by land;
Nor aught of all man's sons escapes from that command.

So from the sally each obeys
The unseen almighty nod;
So till the ending all their ways
Blindfolded loth have trod:
Nor knew their task at all, but were the tools of God.

And as the fervent smith of yore
Beat out the glowing blade,
Nor wielded in the front of war
The weapons that he made,
But in the tower at home still plied his ringing trade;

So like a sword the son shall roam
On nobler missions sent;
And as the smith remained at home
In peaceful turret pent,
So sits the while at home the mother well content.

3
STORIES IN VERSE

Robin and Ben

HEATHER ALE
A Galloway Legend

From the bonny bells of heather
    They brewed a drink long-syne,
Was sweeter far than honey,
    Was stronger far than wine.
They brewed it and they drank it,
    And lay in a blessed swound
For days and days together
    In their dwellings underground.

There rose a king in Scotland,
    A fell man to his foes,
He smote the Picts in battle,
    He hunted them like roes.
Over miles of the red mountain
    He hunted as they fled,
And strewed the dwarfish bodies
    Of the dying and the dead.

Summer came in the country,
    Red was the heather bell;
But the manner of the brewing
    Was none alive to tell.
In graves that were like children's
    On many a mountain head,
The Brewsters of the Heather
    Lay numbered with the dead.

The king in the red moorland
    Rode on a summer's day;
And the bees hummed, and the curlews
    Cried beside the way.
The king rode, and was angry,

Black was his brow and pale,
To rule in a land of heather
    And lack the Heather Ale.

It fortuned that his vassals,
    Riding free on the heath,
Came on a stone that was fallen
    And vermin hid beneath.
Rudely plucked from their hiding,
    Never a word they spoke:
A son and his aged father—
    Last of the dwarfish folk.

The king sat high on his charger,
    He looked on the little men;
And the dwarfish and swarthy couple
    Looked at the king again.
Down by the shore he had them;
    And there on the giddy brink—
'I will give you life, ye vermin,
    For the secret of the drink.'

There stood the son and father
    And they looked high and low;
The heather was red around them,
    The sea rumbled below.
And up and spoke the father,
    Shrill was his voice to hear:
'I have a word in private,
    A word for the royal ear.

'Life is dear to the aged,
    And honour a little thing;
I would gladly sell the secret,'
    Quoth the Pict to the King.

His voice was small as a sparrow's,
    And shrill and wonderful clear:
'I would gladly sell my secret,
    Only my son I fear.

'For life is a little matter,
    And death is nought to the young;
And I dare not sell my honour
    Under the eye of my son.
Take *him*, O king, and bind him,
    And cast him far in the deep;
And it's I will tell the secret
    That I have sworn to keep.'

They took the son and bound him,
    Neck and heels in a thong,
And a lad took him and swung him,
    And flung him far and strong,
And the sea swallowed his body,
    Like that of a child of ten;—
And there on the cliff stood the father,
    Last of the dwarfish men.

'True was the word I told you:
    Only my son I feared;
For I doubt the sapling courage
    That goes without the beard.
But now in vain is the torture,
    Fire shall never avail:
Here dies in my bosom
    The secret of Heather Ale.'

TICONDEROGA
A Legend of the West Highlands

This is the tale of the man
   Who heard a word in the night
In the land of the heathery hills,
   In the days of the feud and the fight.
By the sides of the rainy sea,
   Where never a stranger came,
On the awful lips of the dead,
   He heard the outlandish name.
It sang in his sleeping ears,
   It hummed in his waking head:
The name—Ticonderoga,
   The utterance of the dead.

I. THE SAYING OF THE NAME

On the loch-sides of Appin,
   When the mist blew from the sea,
A Stewart stood with a Cameron:
   An angry man was he.
The blood beat in his ears,
   The blood ran hot to his head,
The mist blew from the sea,
   And there was the Cameron dead.
'O, what have I done to my friend,
   O, what have I done to mysel',
That he should be cold and dead,
   And I in the danger of all?
Nothing but danger about me,
   Danger behind and before,
Death at wait in the heather
   In Appin and Mamore,

Hate at all of the ferries
    And death at each of the fords,
Camerons priming gunlocks
    And Camerons sharpening swords.'

But this was a man of counsel,
    This was a man of a score,
There dwelt no pawkier Stewart
    In Appin or Mamore.
He looked on the blowing mist,
    He looked on the awful dead,
And there came a smile on his face
    And there slipped a thought in his head.

Out over cairn and moss,
    Out over scrog and scaur,
He ran as runs the clansman
    That bears the cross of war.
His heart beat in his body,
    His hair clove to his face,
When he came at last in the gloaming
    To the dead man's brother's place.
The east was white with the moon,
    The west with the sun was red,
And there, in the house-doorway,
    Stood the brother of the dead.

'I have slain a man to my danger,
    I have slain a man to my death.
I put my soul in your hands,'
    The panting Stewart saith.
'I lay it bare in your hands,
    For I know your hands are leal;
And be you my targe and bulwark
    From the bullet and the steel.'

Then up and spoke the Cameron,
    And gave him his hand again:
'There shall never a man in Scotland
    Set faith in me in vain;
And whatever man you have slaughtered,
    Of whatever name or line,
By my sword and yonder mountain,
    I make your quarrel mine.
I bid you in to my fireside,
    I share with you house and hall;
It stands upon my honour
    To see you safe from all.'

It fell in the time of midnight,
    When the fox barked in the den
And the plaids were over the faces
    In all the houses of men,
That as the living Cameron
    Lay sleepless on his bed,
Out of the night and the other world,
    Came in to him the dead.

'My blood is on the heather,
    My bones are on the hill;
There is joy in the home of ravens
    That the young shall eat their fill.
My blood is poured in the dust,
    My soul is spilled in the air;
And the man that has undone me
    Sleeps in my brother's care.'

'I'm wae for your death, my brother,
    But if all of my house were dead,
I couldnae withdraw the plighted hand,
    Nor break the word once said.'

'O, what shall I say to our father,
     In the place to which I fare?
O, what shall I say to our mother,
     Who greets to see me there?
And to all the kindly Camerons
     That have lived and died long-syne—
Is this the word you send them,
     Fause-hearted brother mine?'

'It's neither fear nor duty,
     It's neither quick nor dead
Shall gar me withdraw the plighted hand,
     Or break the word once said.'

Thrice in the time of midnight,
     When the fox barked in the den,
And the plaids were over the faces
     In all the houses of men,
Thrice as the living Cameron
     Lay sleepless on his bed,
Out of the night and the other world
     Came in to him the dead,
And cried to him for vengeance
     On the man that laid him low;
And thrice the living Cameron
     Told the dead Cameron, no.

'Thrice have you seen me, brother,
     But now shall see me no more,
Till you meet your angry fathers
     Upon the farther shore.
Thrice have I spoken, and now,
     Before the cock be heard,
I take my leave for ever

With the naming of a word.
It shall sing in your sleeping ears,
    It shall hum in your waking head,
The name—Ticonderoga,
    And the warning of the dead.'

Now when the night was over
    And the time of people's fears,
The Cameron walked abroad,
    And the word was in his ears.
'Many a name I know,
    But never a name like this;
O, where shall I find a skilly man
    Shall tell me what it is?'
With many a man he counselled
    Of high and low degree,
With the herdsmen on the mountains
    And the fishers of the sea.
And he came and went unweary,
    And read the books of yore,
And the runes that were written of old
    On stones upon the moor.
And many a name he was told,
    But never the name of his fears—
Never, in east or west,
    The name that rang in his ears:
Names of men and of clans;
    Names for the grass and the tree,
For the smallest tarn in the mountains,
    The smallest reef in the sea:
Names for the high and low,
    The names of the craig and the flat;
But in all the land of Scotland,
    Never a name like that.

II. THE SEEKING OF THE NAME

And now there was speech in the south,
    And a man of the south that was wise,
A periwig'd lord of London,
    Called on the clans to rise.
And the riders rode, and the summons
    Came to the western shore,
To the land of the sea and the heather,
    To Appin and Mamore.
It called on all to gather
    From every scrog and scaur,
That loved their fathers' tartan
    And the ancient game of war.

And down the watery valley
    And up the windy hill,
Once more, as in the olden,
    The pipes were sounding shrill;
Again in highland sunshine
    The naked steel was bright;
And the lads, once more in tartan
    Went forth again to fight.

'O, why should I dwell here
    With a weird upon my life,
When the clansmen shout for battle
    And the war-swords clash in strife?
I cannae joy at feast,
    I cannae sleep in bed,
For the wonder of the word
    And the warning of the dead.
It sings in my sleeping ears,
    It hums in my waking head,
The name—Ticonderoga,
    The utterance of the dead.

Then up, and with the fighting men
    To march away from here,
Till the cry of the great war-pipe
    Shall drown it in my ear!'

Where flew King George's ensign
    The plaided soldiers went:
They drew the sword in Germany,
    In Flanders pitched the tent.
The bells of foreign cities
    Rang far across the plain:
They passed the happy Rhine,
    They drank the rapid Main.
Through Asiatic jungles
    The Tartans filed their way,
And the neighing of the war-pipes
    Struck terror in Cathay.

'Many a name have I heard,' he thought,
    'In all the tongues of men,
Full many a name both here and there,
    Full many both now and then.
When I was at home in my father's house
    In the land of the naked knee,
Between the eagles that fly in the lift
    And the herrings that swim in the sea,
And now that I am a captain-man
    With a braw cockade in my hat—
Many a name have I heard,' he thought,
    'But never a name like that.'

III. THE PLACE OF THE NAME

There fell a war in a woody place,
    Lay far across the sea,
A war of the march in the mirk midnight

And the shot from behind the tree,
The shaven head and the painted face,
    The silent foot in the wood,
In a land of a strange, outlandish tongue
    That was hard to be understood.

It fell about the gloaming
    The general stood with his staff,
He stood and he looked east and west
    With little mind to laugh.
'Far have I been and much have I seen,
    And kent both gain and loss,
But here we have woods on every hand
    And a kittle water to cross.
Far have I been and much have I seen,
    But never the beat of this;
And there's one must go down to that waterside
    To see how deep it is.'

It fell in the dusk of the night
    When unco things betide,
The skilly captain, the Cameron,
    Went down to that waterside.
Canny and soft the captain went;
    And a man of the woody land,
With the shaven head and the painted face,
    Went down at his right hand.
It fell in the quiet night,
    There was never a sound to ken;
But all of the woods to the right and the left
    Lay filled with the painted men.

'Far have I been and much have I seen,
    Both as a man and boy,
But never have I set forth a foot

On so perilous an employ.'
It fell in the dusk of the night
    When unco things betide,
That he was aware of a captain-man
    Drew near to the waterside.
He was aware of his coming
    Down in the gloaming alone;
And he looked in the face of the man
    And lo! the face was his own.
'This is my weird,' he said,
    'And now I ken the worst;
For many shall fall the morn,
    But I shall fall with the first.
O, you of the outland tongue,
    You of the painted face,
This is the place of my death;
    Can you tell me the name of the place?'
'Since the Frenchmen have been here
    They have called it Sault-Marie;
But that is a name for priests,
    And not for you and me.
It went by another word,'
    Quoth he of the shaven head:
'It was called Ticonderoga
    In the days of the great dead.'

And it fell on the morrow's morning,
    In the fiercest of the fight,
That the Cameron bit the dust
    As he foretold at night;
And far from the hills of heather
    Far from the isles of the sea,
He sleeps in the place of the name
    As it was doomed to be.

CHRISTMAS AT SEA

The sheets were frozen hard, and they cut the naked hand;
The decks were like a slide, where a seaman scarce
    could stand;
The wind was a nor'wester, blowing squally off the sea;
And cliffs and spouting breakers were the only things a-lee.

They heard the surf a-roaring before the break of day;
But 'twas only with the peep of light we saw how ill we lay.
We tumbled every hand on deck instanter, with a shout,
And we gave her the maintops'l, and stood by to go about.

All day we tacked and tacked between the South Head
    and the North;
All day we hauled the frozen sheets, and got no further
    forth;
All day as cold as charity, in bitter pain and dread,
For very life and nature we tacked from head to head.

We gave the South a wider berth, for there the tide-
    race roared;
But every tack we made we brought the North Head
    close aboard:
So's we saw the cliffs and houses, and the breakers
    running high,
And the coastguard in his garden, with his glass
    against his eye.

The frost was on the village roofs as white as ocean foam;
The good red fires were burning bright in every
    'longshore home;
The windows sparkled clear, and the chimneys volleyed
    out;
And I vow we sniffed the victuals as the vessel went about.

The bells upon the church were rung with a mighty
    jovial cheer;
For it's just that I should tell you how (of all days in the
    year)
This day of our adversity was blessed Christmas morn,
And the house above the coastguard's was the house
    where I was born.

O well I saw the pleasant room, the pleasant faces there,
My mother's silver spectacles, my father's silver hair;
And well I saw the firelight, like a flight of homely elves,
Go dancing round the china-plates that stand upon the
    shelves.

And well I knew the talk they had, the talk that was of me,
Of the shadow on the household and the son that went
    to sea;
And O the wicked fool I seemed, in every kind of way,
To be here and hauling frozen ropes on blessed Christmas
    Day.

They lit the high sea-light, and the dark began to fall.
'All hands to loose topgallant sails,' I heard the captain call.
'By the Lord, she'll never stand it,' our first mate,
    Jackson, cried.
. . . 'It's the one way or the other, Mr. Jackson,' he
    replied.

She staggered to her bearings, but the sails were new
    and good,
And the ship smelt up to windward just as though she
    understood.
As the winter's day was ending, in the entry of the night,
We cleared the weary headland, and passed below the
    light.

And they heaved a mighty breath, every soul on board
but me,
As they saw her nose again pointing handsome out to sea;
But all that I could think of, in the darkness and the cold,
Was just that I was leaving home and my folks were
growing old.

ROBIN AND BEN: OR, THE PIRATE AND THE APOTHECARY

From *Moral Tales*

Come, lend me an attentive ear
A startling moral tale to hear,
Of Pirate Rob and Chemist Ben,
And different destinies of men.

Deep in the greenest of the vales
That nestle near the coast of Wales,
The heaving main but just in view,
Robin and Ben together grew,
Together worked and played the fool,
Together shunned the Sunday school,
And pulled each other's youthful noses
Around the cots, among the roses.

Together but unlike they grew;
Robin was rough, and through and through
Bold, inconsiderate, and manly,
Like some historic Bruce or Stanley.
Ben had a mean and servile soul,
He robbed not, though he often stole.
He sang on Sunday in the choir,
And tamely capped the passing Squire.

At length, intolerant of trammels—
Wild as the wild Bithynian camels,
Wild as the wild sea-eagles—Bob
His widowed dam contrives to rob,
And thus with great originality
Effectuates his personality.
Thenceforth his terror-haunted flight
He follows through the starry night;
And with the early morning breeze,
Behold him on the azure seas.
The master of a trading dandy
Hires Robin for a go of brandy;
And all the happy hills of home
Vanish beyond the fields of foam.

Ben, meanwhile, like a tin reflector,
Attended on the worthy rector;
Opened his eyes and held his breath,
And flattered to the point of death;
And was at last, by that good fairy,
Apprenticed to the Apothecary.

So Ben, while Robin chose to roam,
A rising chemist was at home,
Tended his shop with learned air,
Watered his drugs and oiled his hair,
And gave advice to the unwary,
Like any sleek apothecary.

Meanwhile upon the deep afar
Robin the brave was waging war,
With other tarry desperadoes
About the latitude of Barbadoes.
He knew no touch of craven fear;
His voice was thunder in the cheer;

First, from the main-to'-gallan' high,
The skulking merchantman to spy—
The first to bound upon the deck,
The last to leave the sinking wreck.
His hand was steel, his word was law,
His mates regarded him with awe.
No pirate in the whole profession
Held a more honourable position.

At length, from years of anxious toil,
Bold Robin seeks his native soil;
Wisely arranges his affairs,
And to his native dale repairs.
The Bristol *Swallow* sets him down
Beside the well-remembered town.
He sighs, he spits, he marks the scene,
Proudly he treads the village green;
And, free from pettiness and rancour,
Takes lodgings at the 'Crown and Anchor.'

Strange, when a man so great and good
Once more in his home-country stood,
Strange that the sordid clowns should show
A dull desire to have him go.
His clinging breeks, his tarry hat,
The way he swore, the way he spat,
A certain quality of manner,
Alarming like the pirate's banner—
Something that did not seem to suit all—
Something, O call it bluff, not brutal—
Something at least, howe'er it's called,
Made Robin generally black-balled.

His soul was wounded; proud and glum,
Alone he sat and swigged his rum,

And took a great distaste to men
Till he encountered Chemist Ben.
Bright was the hour and bright the day
That threw them in each other's way;
Glad were their mutual salutations,
Long their respective revelations.
Before the inn in sultry weather
They talked of this and that together;
Ben told the tale of his indentures,
And Rob narrated his adventures.
Last, as the point of greatest weight,
The pair contrasted their estate,
And Robin, like a boastful sailor,
Despised the other for a tailor.

'See,' he remarked, 'with envy, see
A man with such a fist as me!
Bearded and ringed, and big, and brown,
I sit and toss the stingo down.

Hear the gold jingle in my bag—
All won beneath the Jolly Flag!'
Ben moralised and shook his head:
'You wanderers earn and eat your bread.
The foe is found, beats or is beaten,
And, either how, the wage is eaten.
And after all your pully-hauly
Your proceeds look uncommon small-ly.
You had done better here to tarry
Apprentice to the Apothecary.
The silent pirates of the shore
Eat and sleep soft, and pocket more

Than any red, robustious ranger
Who picks his farthings hot from danger.
You clank your guineas on the board;
Mine are with several bankers stored.
You reckon riches on your digits,
You dash in chase of Sals and Bridgets,
You drink and risk delirium tremens,

Your whole estate a common seaman's!
Regard your friend and school companion,
Soon to be wed to Miss Trevanion
(Smooth, honourable, fat and flowery,
With Heaven knows how much land in dowry).
Look at me—am I in good case?
Look at my hands, look at my face;
Look at the cloth of my apparel;
Try me and test me, lock and barrel;
And own, to give the devil his due,
I have made more of life than you.
Yet I nor sought nor risked a life;
I shudder at an open knife;
The perilous seas I still avoided
And stuck to land whate'er betided.
I had no gold, no marble quarry,
I was a poor apothecary,
Yet here I stand, at thirty-eight,
A man of an assured estate.'

'Well,' answered Robin—'well, and how?'

The smiling chemist tapped his brow.
'Rob,' he replied, 'this throbbing brain
Still worked and hankered after gain.
By day and night, to work my will,
It pounded like a powder mill;
And marking how the world went round
A theory of theft it found.
Here is the key to right and wrong:
Steal little, but steal all day long;
And this invaluable plan
Marks what is called the Honest Man.
When first I served with Doctor Pill,
My hand was ever in the till.

Now that I am myself a master,
My gains come softer still and faster.
As thus: on Wednesday, a maid
Came to me in the way of trade.
Her mother, an old farmer's wife,
Required a drug to save her life.
'At once, my dear, at once,' I said,
Patted the child upon the head,
Bade her be still a loving daughter,
And filled the bottle up with water.'

'Well, and the mother?' Robin cried.

'O she!' said Ben—'I think she died.'

'Battle and blood, death and disease,
Upon the tainted Tropic seas—
The attendant sharks that chew the cud—
The abhorred scuppers spouting blood—
The untended dead, the Tropic sun—

The thunder of the murderous gun—
The cut-throat crew—the Captain's curse—
The tempest blustering worse and worse—
These have I known and these can stand,
But you—I settle out of hand!'

Out flashed the cutlass, down went Ben
Dead and rotten, there and then.

4
WORDS AND
WONDERS

The Little Land

HAPPY THOUGHT

The world is so full of a number of things,
I'm sure we should all be as happy as kings.

SINGING

Of speckled eggs the birdie sings
    And nests among the trees;
The sailor sings of ropes and things
    In ships upon the seas.

The children sing in far Japan,
    The children sing in Spain;
The organ with the organ man
    Is singing in the rain.

BRIGHT IS THE RING OF WORDS

Bright is the ring of words
    When the right man rings them,
Fair the fall of songs
    When the singer sings them.
Still they are carolled and said—
    On wings they are carried—
After the singer is dead
    And the maker buried.

Low as the singer lies
    In the field of heather,
Songs of his fashion bring
    The swains together.

And when the west is red
    With the sunset embers,
The lover lingers and sings
    And the maid remembers.

JUMBO AND IBIS
From *Moral Emblems*

See in the print, how moved by whim,
Trumpeting Jumbo, great and grim,
Adjusts his trunk, like a cravat,
To noose that individual's hat.
The sacred Ibis in the distance
Joys to observe his bold resistance.

I WILL MAKE YOU BROOCHES

I will make you brooches and toys for your delight
Of bird-song at morning and star-shine at night.
I will make a palace fit for you and me
Of green days in forests and blue days at sea.

I will make my kitchen, and you shall keep your room,
Where white flows the river and bright blows the broom,
And you shall wash your linen and keep your body white
In rainfall at morning and dewfall at night.

And this shall be for music when no one else is near,
The fine song for singing, the rare song to hear!
That only I remember, that only you admire,
Of the broad road that stretches and the roadside fire.

THE LAND OF COUNTERPANE

When I was sick and lay a-bed,
I had two pillows at my head,
And all my toys beside me lay
To keep me happy all the day.

And sometimes for an hour or so
I watched my leaden soldiers go,
With different uniforms and drills,
Among the bed-clothes, through the hills;

And sometimes sent my ships in fleets
All up and down among the sheets;
Or brought my trees and houses out,
And planted cities all about.

I was the giant great and still
That sits upon the pillow-hill,
And sees before him, dale and plain,
The pleasant land of counterpane.

THE LITTLE LAND

When at home alone I sit
And am very tired of it,
I have just to shut my eyes
To go sailing through the skies—
To go sailing far away
To the pleasant Land of Play;
To the fairy land afar

Where the Little People are;
Where the clover-tops are trees,
And the rain-pools are the seas,
And the leaves, like little ships,
Sail about on tiny trips;
And above the daisy tree
    Through the grasses,
High o'erhead the Bumble Bee
    Hums and passes.

In that forest to and fro
I can wander, I can go;
See the spider and the fly,
And the ants go marching by,
Carrying parcels with their feet
Down the green and grassy street.
I can in the sorrel sit
Where the ladybird alit.
I can climb the jointed grass
    And on high
See the greater swallows pass
    In the sky,
And the round sun rolling by
Heeding no such things as I.

Through that forest I can pass
Till, as in a looking-glass,
Humming fly and daisy tree
And my tiny self I see,
Painted very clear and neat
On the rain-pool at my feet.
Should a leaflet come to land
Drifting near to where I stand,
Straight I'll board that tiny boat
Round the rain-pool sea to float.

Little thoughtful creatures sit
On the grassy coasts of it;
Little things with lovely eyes
See me sailing with surprise.
Some are clad in armour green—
(These have sure to battle been!)—
Some are pied with ev'ry hue,
Black and crimson, gold and blue;
Some have wings and swift are gone;—
But they all look kindly on.

When my eyes I once again
Open, and see all things plain:
High bare walls, great bare floor;
Great big knobs on drawer and door;
Great big people perched on chairs,
Stitching tucks and mending tears,
Each a hill that I could climb,
And talking nonsense all the time—

O dear me,
That I could be
A sailor on the rain-pool sea,
A climber in the clover tree,
And just come back, a sleepy-head,
Late at night to go to bed.

THE LAND OF STORY-BOOKS

At evening when the lamp is lit,
Around the fire my parents sit;
They sit at home and talk and sing,
And do not play at anything.

Now, with my little gun, I crawl
All in the dark along the wall,
And follow round the forest track
Away behind the sofa back.

There, in the night, where none can spy,
All in my hunter's camp I lie,
And play at books that I have read
Till it is time to go to bed.

These are the hills, these are the woods,
These are my starry solitudes;
And there the river by whose brink
The roaring lions come to drink.

I see the others far away
As if in firelit camp they lay,
And I, like to an Indian scout,
Around their party prowled about.

So when my nurse comes in for me,
Home I return across the sea,
And go to bed with backward looks
At my dear land of Story-books.

ESCAPE AT BEDTIME

The lights from the parlour and kitchen shone out
    Through the blinds and the windows and bars;
And high overhead and all moving about,
    There were thousands of millions of stars.
There ne'er were such thousands of leaves on a tree,
    Nor of people in church or the Park,
As the crowds of the stars that looked down upon me,
    And that glittered and winked in the dark.

The Dog, and the Plough, and the Hunter, and all,
    And the star of the sailor, and Mars,
These shone in the sky, and the pail by the wall
    Would be half full of water and stars.
They saw me at last, and they chased me with cries,
    And they soon had me packed into bed;
But the glory kept shining and bright in my eyes,
    And the stars going round in my head.

THE MOON

The moon has a face like the clock in the hall;
She shines on thieves on the garden wall,
On streets and fields and harbour quays,
And birdies asleep in the forks of the trees.

The squalling cat and the squeaking mouse,
The howling dog by the door of the house,
The bat that lies in bed at noon,
All love to be out by the light of the moon.

But all of the things that belong to the day
Cuddle to sleep to be out of her way;
And flowers and children close their eyes
Till up in the morning the sun shall arise.

THE LAND OF NOD

From breakfast on through all the day
At home among my friends I stay,
But every night I go abroad
Afar into the Land of Nod.

All by myself I have to go,
With none to tell me what to do—
All alone beside the streams
And up the mountain-sides of dreams.

The strangest things are there for me,
Both things to eat and things to see,
And many frightening sights abroad
Till morning in the Land of Nod.

Try as I like to find the way,
I never can get back by day,
Nor can remember plain and clear
The curious music that I hear.

YOUNG NIGHT-THOUGHT

All night long and every night,
When my mama puts out the light,
I see the people marching by,
As plain as day before my eye.

Armies and emperor and kings,
All carrying different kinds of things,
And marching in so grand a way,
You never saw the like by day.

So fine a show was never seen
At the great circus on the green;
For every kind of beast and man
Is marching in that caravan.

As first they move a little slow,
But still the faster on they go,
And still beside me close I keep
Until we reach the town of Sleep.

WINDY NIGHTS

Whenever the moon and stars are set,
   Whenever the wind is high,
All night long in the dark and wet,
   A man goes riding by.
Late in the night when the fires are out,
Why does he gallop and gallop about?

Whenever the trees are crying aloud,
    And ships are tossed at sea,
By, on the highway, low and loud,
    By at the gallop goes he.
By at the gallop he goes, and then
By he comes back at the gallop again.

TIME TO RISE

A birdie with a yellow bill
Hopped upon my window sill,
Cocked his shining eye and said:
'Ain't you 'shamed, you sleepy-head?'

MY SHADOW

I have a little shadow that goes in and out with me,
And what can be the use of him is more than I can see.
He is very, very like me from the heels up to the head;
And I see him jump before me, when I jump into my bed.

The funniest thing about him is the way he likes to grow—
Not at all like proper children, which is always very slow;
For he sometimes shoots up taller like an india-rubber ball,
And he sometimes gets so little that there's none of
        him at all.

He hasn't got a notion of how children ought to play,
And can only make a fool of me in every sort of way.
He stays so close beside me, he's a coward you can see;
I'd think shame to stick to nursie as that shadow sticks
        to me!

One morning, very early, before the sun was up,
I rose and found the shining dew on every buttercup;
But my lazy little shadow, like an arrant sleepy-head,
Had stayed at home behind me and was fast asleep in bed.

THE HOUSE BEAUTIFUL

A naked house, a naked moor,
A shivering pool before the door,
A garden bare of flowers and fruit
And poplars at the garden foot:
Such is the place that I live in,
Bleak without and bare within.

Yet shall your ragged moor receive
The incomparable pomp of eve,
And the cold glories of the dawn
Behind your shivering trees be drawn;
And when the wind from place to place
Doth the unmoored cloud-galleons chase,
Your garden gloom and gleam again,
With leaping sun, with glancing rain.
Here shall the wizard moon ascend
The heavens, in the crimson end
Of day's declining splendour; here
The army of the stars appear.
The neighbour hollows dry or wet,
Spring shall with tender flowers beset;
And oft the morning muser see
Larks rising from the broomy lea,
And every fairy wheel and thread
Of cobweb dew-bediamonded.

When daisies go, shall winter time
Silver the simple grass with rime;
Autumnal frosts enchant the pool
And make the cart-ruts beautiful;
And when snow-bright the moor expands,
How shall your children clap their hands!
To make this earth, our hermitage,
A cheerful and a changeful page,
God's bright and intricate device
Of days and seasons doth suffice.

5
COAST AND SEA

The Light-Keeper

I SIT UP HERE AT MIDNIGHT

I sit up here at midnight,
    The wind is in the street,
The rain besieges the windows
    Like the sound of many feet.

I see the street lamps flicker,
    I see them wink and fail,
The streets are wet and empty,
    It blows an easterly gale.

Some think of the fisher skipper
    Beyond the Inchcape stone;
But I of the fisher woman
    That lies at home alone.

She raises herself on her elbow
    And watches the firelit floor;
Her eyes are bright with terror,
    Her heart beats fast and sore.

Between the roar of the flurries,
    When the tempest holds his breath
She holds her breathing also—
    It is all as still as death.

She can hear the cinders dropping,
    The cat that purrs in its sleep—
The foolish fisher woman!
    Her heart is on the deep.

A VISIT FROM THE SEA

Far from the loud sea beaches
    Where he goes fishing and crying,
Here in the inland garden
    Why is the sea-gull flying?

Here are no fish to dive for;
    Here is the corn and lea;
Here are the green trees rustling.
    Hie away home to sea!

Fresh is the river water
    And quiet among the rushes;
This is no home for the sea-gull
    But for the rooks and thrushes.

Pity the bird that has wandered!
    Pity the sailor ashore!
Hurry him home to the ocean,
    Let him come here no more!

High on the sea-cliff ledges
    The white gulls are trooping and crying,
Here among rooks and roses,
    Why is the sea-gull flying?

SKERRYVORE: THE PARALLEL

Here all is sunny, and when the truant gull
Skims the green level of the lawn, his wing
Dispetals roses; here the house is framed
Of kneaded brick and the plumed mountain pine,

Such clay as artists fashion and such wood
As the tree-climbing urchin breaks. But there
Eternal granite hewn from the living isle
And dowelled with brute iron, rears a tower
That from its wet foundation to its crown
Of glittering glass, stands, in the sweep of winds,
Immovable, immortal, eminent.

THE LIGHT-KEEPER

I

The brilliant kernel of the night,
The flaming lightroom circles me:
I sit within a blaze of light
Held high above the dusky sea.
Far off the surf doth break and roar
Along bleak miles of moonlit shore,
Where through the tides the tumbling wave
Falls in an avalanche of foam
And drives its churned waters home
Up many an undercliff and cave.

The clear bell chimes: the clockworks strain,
The turning lenses flash and pass,
Frame turning within glittering frame
With frosty gleam of moving glass:
Unseen by me, each dusky hour
The sea-waves welter up the tower
Or in the ebb subside again;
And ever and anon all night,
Drawn from afar by charm of light,
A sea bird beats against the pane.

And lastly when dawn ends the night
And belts the semi-orb of sea,
The tall, pale pharos in the light
Looks white and spectral as may be.
The early ebb is out: the green
Straight belt of seaweed now is seen,
That round the basement of the tower
Marks out the interspace of tide;
And watching men are heavy-eyed,
And sleepless lips are dry and sour.

The night is over like a dream:
The sea-birds cry and dip themselves:
And in the early sunlight, steam

The newly bared and dripping shelves,
Around whose verge the glassy wave
With lisping wash is heard to lave;
While, on the white tower lifted high,
The circling lenses flash and pass
With yellow light in faded glass
And sickly shine against the sky.

II

As the steady lenses circle
With a frosty gleam of glass;
And the clear bell chimes,
And the oil brims over the lip of the burner,
Quiet and still at his desk,
The lonely Light-Keeper
Holds his vigil.

Lured from far,
The bewildered seagull beats
Dully against the lantern;
Yet he stirs not, lifts not his head
From the desk where he reads,
Lifts not his eyes to see
The chill blind circle of night
Watching him through the panes.
This is his country's guardian,
The outmost sentry of peace.
This is the man
Who gives up that is lovely in living
For the means to live.

Poetry cunningly gilds
The life of the Light-Keeper,
Held on high in the blackness
In the burning kernel of night,

The seaman sees and blesses him,
The Poet, deep in a sonnet,
Numbers his inky fingers
Fitly to praise him.
Only we behold him,
Sitting, patient and stolid,
Martyr to a salary.

SING ME A SONG OF A LAD THAT IS GONE

Sing me a song of a lad that is gone,
    Say, could that lad be I?
Merry of soul he sailed on a day
    Over the sea to Skye.

Mull was astern, Rum on the port,
    Eigg on the starboard bow;
Glory of youth glowed in his soul:
    Where is that glory now?

Sing me a song of a lad that is gone,
    Say, could that lad be I?
Merry of soul he sailed on a day
    Over the sea to Skye.

Give me again all that was there,
    Give me the sun that shone!
Give me the eyes, give me the soul,
    Give me the lad that's gone!

Sing me a song of a lad that is gone,
    Say, could that lad be I?
Merry of soul he sailed on a day
    Over the sea to Skye.

Billow and breeze, islands and seas,
    Mountains of rain and sun,
All that was good, all that was fair,
    All that was me is gone.

6
SONGS
OF TRAVEL

From a Railway-Carriage

TRAVEL

I should like to rise and go
Where the golden apples grow;
Where below another sky
Parrot islands anchored lie,
And, watched by cockatoos and goats,
Lonely Crusoes building boats;
Where in sunshine reaching out
Eastern cities, miles about,
Are with mosque and minaret
Among sandy gardens set,
And the rich goods from near and far
Hang for sale in the bazaar;
Where the Great Wall round China goes,
And on one side the desert blows,
And with bell and voice and drum,
Cities on the other hum;
Where are forests hot as fire,
Wide as England, tall as a spire,
Full of apes and cocoa-nuts
And the negro hunters' huts;
Where the knotty crocodile
Lies and blinks in the Nile,
And the red flamingo flies
Hunting fish before his eyes;
Where in jungles near and far,
Man-devouring tigers are,
Lying close and giving ear
Lest the hunt be drawing near,
Or a comer-by be seen
Swinging in a palanquin;
Where among the desert sands
Some deserted city stands,

All its children, sweep and prince,
Grown to manhood ages since,
Not a foot in street or house,
Not a stir of child or mouse,
And when kindly falls the night,
In all the town no spark of light.
There I'll come when I'm a man
With a camel caravan;
Light a fire in the gloom
Of some dusty dining-room;
See the pictures on the walls,
Heroes, fights and festivals;
And in a corner find the toys
Of the old Egyptian boys.

A CAMP
From *Travels with a Donkey*

The bed was made, the room was fit,
By punctual eve the stars were lit;
The air was still, the water ran,
No need was there for maid or man,
When we put up, my ass and I,
At God's green caravanserai.

THE INFINITE SHINING HEAVENS

The infinite shining heavens
    Rose and I saw in the night
Uncountable angel stars
    Showering sorrow and light.

I saw them distant as heaven,
    Dumb and shining and dead,
And the idle stars of the night
    Were dearer to me than bread.

Night after night in my sorrow
    The stars stood over the sea,
Till lo! I looked in the dusk
    And a star had come down to me.

FROM A RAILWAY CARRIAGE

Faster than fairies, faster than witches,
Bridges and houses, hedges and ditches;
And charging along like troops in a battle
All through the meadows the horses and cattle:
All of the sights of the hill and the plain
Fly as thick as driving rain;
And ever again, in the wink of an eye,
Painted stations whistle by.

Here is a child who clambers and scrambles,
All by himself and gathering brambles;
Here is a tramp who stands and gazes;
And here is the green for stringing the daisies!
Here is a cart run away in the road
Lumping along with man and load;
And here is a mill, and there is a river:
Each a glimpse and gone forever!

7
AMERICA

Winter

THE SUN'S TRAVELS

The sun is not a-bed, when I
At night upon my pillow lie;
Still round the earth his way he takes,
And morning after morning makes.

While here at home, in shining day,
We round the sunny garden play,
Each little Indian sleepy-head
Is being kissed and put to bed.

And when at eve I rise from tea,
Day dawns beyond the Atlantic Sea;
And all the children in the West
Are getting up and being dressed.

IN THE STATES

With half a heart I wander here
    As from an age gone by
A brother—yet though young in years.
    An elder brother, I.

You speak another tongue than mine,
    Though both were English born.
I towards the night of time decline,
    You mount into the morn.

Youth shall grow great and strong and free,
    But age must still decay:
To-morrow for the States—for me,
    England and Yesterday.

OF WHERE OR HOW, I NOTHING KNOW

Of where or how, I nothing know,
    And why I do not care.
    Enough if even so,
My travelling eyes, my travelling mind can go
By flood and field and hill, by wood and meadow fair,
Beside the Susquehanna and along the Delaware.

I think, I hope, I dream no more
    The dreams of otherwhere,
    The cherished thoughts of yore;
I have been changed from what I was before;
Or breathed perchance too deep the lotus of the air
Beside the Susquehanna and along the Delaware.

Though westward steers the train, my soul
    Shall for the East declare;
    Shall take the East for goal,
Outward and upward bound; and still shall roll,
And still unconquered live, as now she spurns despair
Beside the Susquehanna and along the Delaware.

Unweary God me yet shall bring
    To lands of brighter air,
    Where I, now half a king,
Shall with superior spirit loudlier sing,
And wear a bolder front than that which now I wear
Beside the Susquehanna and along the Delaware.

WINTER

In rigorous hours, when down the iron lane
The redbreast looks in vain
For hips and haws,
Lo, shining flowers upon my window-pane
The silver pencil of the winter draws.

When all the snowy hill
And the bare woods are still;
When snipes are silent in the frozen bogs,
And all the garden garth is whelmed in mire,
Lo, by the hearth, the laughter of the logs—
More fair than roses, lo, the flowers of fire!

Written at Saranac Lake in the Adirondack
Mountains, upstate New York

FAREWELL, AND WHEN FORTH

Farewell, and when forth
I through the Golden Gates to Golden Isles
Steer without smiling, through the sea of smiles,
Isle upon isle, in the seas of the south,
Isle upon island, sea upon sea,
Why should I sail, why should the breeze?
I have been young, and I have counted friends.
A hopeless sail I spread, too late, too late.
Why should I from isle to isle
Sail, a hopeless sailor?

8
ISLAND ADVENTURES

Far Over Seas an Island Is

FAIR ISLE AT SEA

Fair Isle at Sea—thy lovely name
Soft in my ear like music came.
That sea I loved, and once or twice
I touched at isles of Paradise.

FAR OVER SEAS AN ISLAND IS

Far over seas an island is
    Whereon when day is done
A grove of tossing palms
    Are printed on the sun.
And all about the reefy shore
    Blue breakers flash and fall.
There shall I go, methinks,
    When I am done with all.

Have I no castle then in Spain,
    No island of the mind,
Where I can turn and go again
    When life shall prove unkind.
Up, sluggard soul! and far from here
    Our mountain forest seek;
Or nigh the enchanted island, steer
    Down the desirèd creek.

PIRATE DITTY
From *Treasure Island*

Fifteen men on the Dead Man's Chest—
    Yo-ho-ho, and a bottle of rum!
Drink and the devil had done for the rest—
    Yo-ho-ho, and a bottle of rum!

TO PRINCESS KAIULANI

[Written in April to Kaiulani in the April of her
age; and at Waikiki, within easy walk of Kaiulani's
banyan!

When she comes to my land and her father's,
and the rain beats upon the window (as I fear it
will), let her look at this page; it will be like a weed
gathered and pressed at home; and she will remember her own islands, and the shadow of the
mighty tree; and she will hear the peacocks screaming in the dusk and the wind blowing in the palms;
and she will think of her father sitting there
alone.—R. L. S.]

    Forth from her land to mine she goes,
    The island maid, the island rose,
    Light of heart and bright of face:
    The daughter of a double race.

    Her islands here, in Southern sun,
    Shall mourn their Kaiulani gone,
    And I, in her dear banyan shade,
    Look vainly for my little maid.

But our Scots islands far away
Shall glitter with unwonted day,
And cast for once their tempests by
To smile in Kaiulani's eye.

Honolulu.

9
HOME THOUGHTS
FROM ABROAD

Requiem

TO THE TUNE OF WANDERING WILLIE

Home no more home to me, whither must I wander?
    Hunger my driver, I go where I must.
Cold blows the winter wind over hill and heather;
    Thick drives the rain, and my roof is in the dust.
Loved of wise men was the shade of my roof-tree.
    The true word of welcome was spoken in the door—
Dear days of old, with the faces in the firelight,
    Kind folks of old, you come again no more.

Home was home then, my dear, full of kindly faces,
    Home was home then, my dear, happy for the child.
Fire and the windows bright glittered on the moorland;
    Song, tuneful song, built a palace in the wild.
Now, when day dawns on the brow of the moorland,
    Lone stands the house, and the chimney-stone is cold.
Lone let it stand, now the friends are all departed,
    The kind hearts, the true hearts, that loved the place
        of old.

Spring shall come, come again, calling up the moorfowl,
    Spring shall bring the sun and rain, bring the bees
        and flowers;
Red shall the heather bloom over hill and valley,
    Soft flow the stream through the even-flowing hours;
Fair the day shine as it shone on my childhood—
    Fair shine the day on the house with open door;
Birds come and cry there and twitter in the chimney—
    But I go for ever and come again no more.

TO S. R. CROCKETT
On receiving a Dedication

Blows the wind today, and the sun and the rain are flying,
    Blows the wind on the moors today and now,
Where about the graves of the martyrs the whaups are
      crying,
    My heart remembers how!

Grey recumbent tombs of the dead in desert places,
    Standing-stones on the vacant wine-red moor,
Hills of sheep, and the howes of the silent vanished races,
    And winds, austere and pure:

Be it granted me to behold you again in dying,
    Hills of home! and to hear again the call;
Hear about the graves of the martyrs the peewees crying,
    And hear no more at all.

Vailima.

REQUIEM

Under the wide and starry sky,
Dig the grave and let me lie.
Glad did I live and gladly die,
    And I laid me down with a will.

This be the verse you grave for me:
Here he lies where he longed to be;
Home is the sailor, home from sea,
    And the hunter home from the hill.

GLOSSARY OF UNFAMILIAR WORDS

ance—once
Auld Reekie—nickname for Edinburgh; means 'Old Smokey'
ayont—beyond

banyan—a fig-tree whose branches take root
black-balled—shunned; rejected; treated as an outcast
brander—grill; broil

caravanserai—an Eastern inn where groups of travellers rest
cauld—cold
chitterin—chattering/shivering with the cold
claes—clothes

daw—dawn
delirium tremens—an illness caused by drinking too much alcohol
dip—a tallow candle

erst—formerly
evenfa'—beginning of the evening; sunset

farthing—an old coin which was worth very little
fraw—from

gaed—went
gang—go

gey an' easy spierin'—very easy to ask
gowsty—windy; gusty

hie—high
howes—hollows; wide plains bounded by hills

kye—cattle

lave—remainder

muckle—big

owre—over

palanquin—a kind of hammock, supported on poles
peewees—lapwings
pharos—a lighthouse
pree—taste

raw—row
Reekie—see *Auld Reekie*

siller—silver; money
spa—a health resort where the mineral water, from a
    spring, is good for you
spaewife—a female fortune-teller
spierin'—see *gey an' easy spierin*
swains—young men living and working in the coun-
    tryside

toddy—a mixture of whisky, sugar (or honey) and hot
    water

whaups—curlews